WHEN YOU
LIVE IN A BUS

JARED ALLEN

WHEN YOU LIVE IN A BUS

LIFE FROM WHERE I'M STANDING

TATE PUBLISHING
AND **ENTERPRISES**, LLC

Published by Tate Publishing & Enterprises, LLC
127 E. Trade Center Terrace | Mustang, Oklahoma 73064 USA
1.888.361.9473 | www.tatepublishing.com

Tate Publishing is committed to excellence in the publishing industry. The company reflects the philosophy established by the founders, based on Psalm 68:11,
"The Lord gave the word and great was the company of those who published it."

Book design copyright © 2016 by Tate Publishing, LLC. All rights reserved.
Cover design by Joana Quilantang
Interior design by Richell Balansag

Published in the United States of America

ISBN: 978-1-68333-546-7
1. Religion / Christian Life / Family
2. Biography & Autobiography / Religious
16.04.19

To Stephen Dodd,
my friend, my mentor in writing, and my inspiration

Contents

Preface 9

A Bit of Introduction 17

About the Bus 23

About Me 35

About My Family 51

Stories 67

Preface

Ever since I was born, I have lived in a bus. It is all I have ever known, the only life I have been accustomed to. Living in a bus is a vastly different dimension than what one might expect. There are so many things that seem normal to me that you might call weird. I was given an extraordinary privilege to have lived my life in a bus, and one of the results of that privilege is my 100 percent unique outlook on life. My worldview (or perspective) has been fashioned since the day of my birth; and because I do live in a bus, traveling and singing with my family, and because I am a Christian and an introverted writer, I have a perspective unlike any other.

As you might expect, I have accumulated hundreds of stories in my lifetime. Though it has been difficult for me to write down these stories—mostly because what interests others about my life is just that, my life—I don't see anything unnatural or intriguing about the way I live. However, upon the encouragement and poignant advice of some dear friends, I will endeavor to tell you the story of my life.

When I was born, I knew there was something different about me from any other person on earth—that is, not including my thumbprint and DNA and whatnot. I was not simply different in the way that each human is different from all others, but rather, I was unique and would stand out because of the situation into which I was born. God placed me in a family who, at the time of my birth, was living in Michigan. My dad—whom I would grow up to love and respect for his wisdom and skill with a "rod of correction," which in my day was known as a belt—was the pastor of a growing congregation at a church in Waterford. My mom was busy at home taking care of myself and my three older siblings: Caleb, Gabrielle, and Josh. Though my dad was a pastor of a church, this life did not last very long for our family. However, and though the small church was growing rapidly and it seemed that the family was just becoming settled, we had just purchased a nice house with a large backyard—something did not sit well in my dad's spirit.

Months went by, and still there was unrest in his spirit. For some reason, he did not understand, or perhaps did not want to understand. Dad felt the call to go into evangelism. He did not understand it because his ministry at the church was growing, and after the recent move to this new house, he knew he could not tell my mom how he felt about things. It would not be fair to her or us children. So he put it off for a while longer, but after several months of wrestling with what he knew was God's will for his life and the lives of his wife and children, he finally gave in. He told my mom how he felt that God was calling him into full-time evangelism and how he had been afraid to say anything to her about it. To his surprise, my mom responded that she had felt the same way but had been too afraid to say anything to him.

Not long after that, we stepped out or, rather, rolled out in faith. Now, at this point, we didn't have a nice forty-five-foot-long bus like we do now. We traveled in a fifth wheel and had only two bookings on our calendar, one right after the other, and nothing else. I was four months old at the time and had contracted a nasty case of the chicken pox, which caught on to the other children rather quickly. Everyone who knew Dad thought he was crazy, and he probably was, but God seems to use the people whom others think are crazy for great things. Just look at Noah. He built a boat in a place that had never seen rain, and not just any boat, one that could fit two of most every animal on earth and five of each clean animal (ones fit to eat and offer as sacrifices). I'll bet everyone on earth outside of his own family thought he was crazy.

That is how our ministry began, with a call from God and obedience on my parents' part. Since then, it has grown far beyond anything they could have ever imagined, and for that, we give God all the glory. The ministry has morphed along the way from primarily preaching to primarily singing—for some divine purpose, each of us children have been blessed with a voice—and that has built upon the dynamic of our mission quite a bit. We went from a fifth wheel to a van and trailer to a motor home to a bigger motor home to a bus.

Things changed quite a bit over the years; our interests changed. Once upon a time, we had a grand collection of stuffed animals with which the older kids would put on "shows" for the younger. I remember the Joe and Edgar Allan Poe show; it was a favorite of us younger kids and lasted several years before we lost one of the stuffed animals. Joe and Edgar Allan Poe were two identical hedgehogs that were both played by Caleb and were impossible to tell apart. Their show mainly consisted of outrageous situations and comedic timing to say the dumbest thing at the perfect time, to which the younger kids would laugh hysterically. Most of the shows were set in the same place and were formatted in the grand tradition of *The Andy Griffith Show* or really any sitcom.

We used to do shows with the old VeggieTales stuffed toys as well, which required a greater imagination as veggies had no arms, legs, or heads really. Some of them, like Bob the Tomato and Madame Blueberry, were just heads and had no body. Talk about traumatizing to a child. Anyway, in one of our very first motor homes, we had lamps that hung from the wall. These lamps hung upside down, which meant that the flower-shaped glass bowl that reflected the light of the bulb faced the ceiling. These lamp bowls were just big enough to conceal perfectly one of the plastic bead-stuffed French peas. One night, when the older kids were putting on a show out front, one of the peas—Jean Claude, I think—was placed up in one of these light bowls when the light was off. When the show was over, we all went to bed and forgot about him.

But in the morning, when the lamps were turned on, we thought something smelled strange, like it was burning. It didn't take us long to pinpoint the location of the smell and figure out what it was that was burning. It was the French pea. The poor fellow had been left in the lamp bowl and got his rear end burned right through. Needless to say, we were distraught. You couldn't have Philippe without Jean Claude. However, after a quick surgical procedure, Jean Claude was as good as new. True, he had a few less plastic beads in him, and he possessed a row of stitches on his posterior, but that didn't seem to matter too much to us.

That was one of the only memories I have of the old motor home, probably because I was only four years old when it happened. But we soon outgrew the little thing, and by the time the family had grown to eight members (six kids and Mom and Dad), we decided to get a bus. Now a bus is a large, rectangular, metal box that has anywhere from eight to ten wheels and can seat at least forty but can comfortably house up to twelve people at any given time. This was the type of bus we bought. Only, when we purchased our first bus, it was a stripped-down passenger coach. Over time, we built it up from nothing as we traveled along.

So, for the beginning parts of traveling in the new bus, there was practically nothing—no finished floor, no carpet, no couches, beds, curtains, sinks, bathrooms, microwaves, or refrigerators. We slept on inflatable pool rafts, air mattresses, or thick piles of blankets packed next to each other in the open space called the front room. It was an interesting couple of months in transition. Dad would have to park at a place with an accessible restroom during the nights such as Walmart or a gas station, and we ate out a lot because there was no way to keep food fresh in the bus, let alone prepare it.

There was one time when we purchased a microwave for the bus (it was the only appliance in the bus at the time and had to sit on the floor because we had no counter), and we happened to be in Pennsylvania at the time. So Dad and

Mom decided to take the family to Hershey's Chocolate World. We had a blast as young kids walking around a chocolate factory—we brought back lots of candy. Giving no thought to where we would keep the candy, we ended up leaving it in the microwave. That night, when everyone was asleep, Mom thought she heard something, so she woke Dad and told him that it sounded like paper rustling. Dad told her it was nothing, and they went back to bed. In the morning, they looked in the microwave to find that a mouse had snuck in and had taken a bite out of every different chocolate bar in there. Not just content with eating one, he felt the need to take a bite out of each different one. So all the chocolate was essentially ruined, and there was no mouse to be found anywhere.

Dad laid out traps and all manner of devices to catch the thing, but he got away every time. He left a trap out one day, and we went in to perform a concert. When we came back, the bait was gone, but the mouse was still around. Dad laid out poison the next time, and we went into another church to perform. When we came out of the church, the mouse was lying outside the bus, dead. He probably ate the poison and then went outside to die.

Slowly but surely, more and more conveniences began to be added to the bus: electricity, running water, couches, beds, and whatnot. Soon it began to look like a home. Living like we did taught me how to do without certain things. I realized that what we call necessities are really just comforts, frills. But life moved on from there. As the family grew, so did the ministry, and the buses grew larger and nicer as God blessed my parents' faithfulness. From then until now has been an interesting journey, but that is how it all came to be.

So this project was written to help others view life from a different perspective and ultimately bring glory and honor to God the Father. I hope you enjoy it.

A Bit of Introduction

I'm a human, right? I have two arms, two legs, a head with a face on it. I mean, it's not like I have claws or wings or multiple sets of eyes or anything. So why do people treat me as if I am an alien from a different planet? Okay, so perhaps it isn't quite that bad, but people do view me differently. But why is that? One answer might be that, to them, I probably appear as some strange phenomenon that they have never seen before now. And why is it that they should view me any different than they view you? Well, no matter who you are or what lifestyle you lead—unless you are one of my siblings—there is a difference between me and you. That difference is that I live in a bus, as in a large, rectangle, metal on wheels, albeit a very nice metal rectangle with several windows, a few couches, a kitchen, and beds enough for the nine people who live in it. Yes, that's the kind of bus that I live in. And not only on weekends like most other professional singers or when my family wants to take a vacation—no, I live in a bus all year long, as in 365 days every year. Approximately 8,760 hours or 525,600 minutes a year, it is my home. And if you find that bizarre, intriguing, crazy, or even scary, this was written just for you.

When you live in a bus, people think strange thoughts about you. When people think strange thoughts about you, they ask you strange questions. When people ask you strange questions, you give them strange answers.

This is the reason that most people misunderstand just what it's like to live in a bus full-time. The misconception here is *because it is different, it must be bad*.

This is, of course, false. Dogs vary from one breed to another, but just because a husky has a different coat than a retriever does not make it any less of a dog. Now, I'm not saying that every person on earth is bound to misunderstand me or think myself and my family strange, but the truth is, the vast majority of people consider it at least slightly odd for a family to live in a bus all the time. But it is the domino effect, or a better term would be the "if you give a mouse a cookie" effect. Simply stated, if you were to give a mouse a cookie, he would not be satisfied with just the cookie, he would also ask for a glass of milk. This, in turn, would not satisfy the mouse any more than the cookie did. He would then ask for a mirror so he could see his milk mustache, and so on.

However effective this method may be, it has flaws. One of the largest being that one question leads to another, which in turn leads to another. This causes the questions to follow a single and rather close-minded path. And even that is not an issue if the first question was the perfect one. For example, if I were to ask you what kind of food you ate for lunch—and let's say that you had pizza—then I asked what kind of pizza, and you said sausage, and I kept asking questions about your lunch and pizza in general. I really don't get to know much about you or who you are. In fact, I have learned nothing about you besides the fact that you prefer sausage pizza to pepperoni.

So you begin to see a little of why people cannot wrap their minds around who I am and what I do. They base their questions on the preconceived notion that living in a bus is strange, and from that perspective, it becomes impossible to ask the right questions. And if they don't ask the right questions, how can they ever know anything about me?

When You Live in a Bus, You Do Things Differently

Some things just cannot be done in the same way on a bus as they would be in a stationary location. For instance, taking a shower. We have two bathrooms on the bus, or what Mom calls one and a half bathrooms. The *half* part just means that one bathroom has a shower and the other does not. People often ask us how we share two bathrooms between nine people. The answer is—we don't. Bathrooms on the bus are operated on a first-come, first-serve basis. If you don't get in way before you need to, you may not get in at all.

But back to showers. If you were in a house, one that didn't move, and you were to take a shower, you could do so without waiting in a long line of people or having to go outside to the water tank and check to make sure you had sufficient water to take a shower. On a bus, however, being in the shower when we are driving (which is majority of the time) could be considered an extreme sport. If you can imagine being on a pogo stick in an earthquake, then you can imagine how it feels to take a shower on a moving bus.

You know it's a bad shower when your body acts like a seismograph meter, and you can tell how many potholes there are by how many times your head hits the ceiling.

You experience many different types of roads—some better, some worse—when living your life in a bus. Though, after twenty years, I'd say that I have grown accustomed to the bumps and jolts of crazy country roads. Every now and again, I come across a road that catches me by surprise, but the army showers are what give me the most trouble. For those of you who are not familiar with the phrase, to take an army shower means that you conserve every bit of water possible, knowing you have a limited amount.

A typical army shower involved you turning the water on and rinsing off, turning the water off and applying soap and shampoo, turning the water back on and rinsing off again. The necessity for quick and frugal showers happens often when you live in a bus. I can think of several times through the years when we were on the road driving to a Sunday morning concert, and most everyone needed a shower. And because no one had the foresight to take one the night before, we had to take army showers; so we would ration the water and get in and out as quickly as possible. It is not the most relaxing way to take a shower, and the bumps and jolts were still present as well. It just comes with the ministry. Some sacrifices have to be made in order for this life to work, and we are all more than happy to make those sacrifices. Not to say we enjoyed the results of those sacrifices. I would take an unmoving shower over one that feels like I'm in a tornado simulator any day.

Now I said that when you live in a bus, you do things differently, and showers are not the only things to which I referred. You have to sleep in a large, rectangular box, five feet off the ground, in a perpetual motion chamber. You will not find a thrill ride at any amusement park as extreme as the experience of sleeping on a moving bus. When this experience was still relatively new, many of us got vertigo so bad that it felt like being on a roller coaster even after we had stopped driving. Some of us had a half wall on our bunks, and others were completely open-faced. When we were all much younger and Dad drove around a sharp turn, these bunks became ramps that oftentimes were so steep that we ended up rolling off them and piling on top of one another on the floor. But that was before we purchased a bus with air pressure control that automatically leveled itself as best it could when such treacherous turns occurred. The bunks were comfortable, perhaps even too comfortable, as it took a great deal of determination to get out of them in the morning.

Our mornings generally happen later in the day because of the amount of willpower it takes to get out from under several warm, cozy blankets and off a bed (which in my case is at the top of the bunks, making it five feet off the ground) and climb down into a cold hallway. We keep the hallway cold not so much for the sake of the cold air but because we have grown so accustomed to the noise of the motor on the bus that we cannot get to sleep without a noise of some kind. The AC unit provides such a noise, and so it is left on all night. And when you bury yourself beneath blankets, you have to keep the air cold. So it is very cold in the mornings. And if you are in an adventurous mood or perhaps are just very hungry, you might even attempt walking out front on the tile floor without socks or slippers on. Usually, the space heater is left out front at night, and whoever wakes up first turns it on to hopefully warm themselves and the floor before the others wake up. This is an everyday routine, though who wakes up first varies from day to day.

About the Bus

I live in a forty-five-foot-long, charcoal gray, eight-wheeled, metal rectangle known as a bus. Now a bus is not a motor home or an RV, at least the one I live in is not. The bus that I live in is more like a house on wheels. Not a mobile home but an actual house built inside of a fifty-passenger tour bus. Literally, the bus I live in was once a tour bus, like the ones people take when they go on "adult field trips" (for lack of a better name).

Obviously, we couldn't just live on a fifty-passenger tour bus. Those seats might be comfortable, but they make terrible microwaves and refrigerators. So we gutted the inside and built/had others build it from the ground up.

Living in a bus has many advantages: you get to see a lot of beautiful landscapes, meet new people every day, and visit exciting new places all across the country. But in equal proportion to the advantages are the disadvantages.

When You Live in a Bus, You Are Constantly Fixing Things

It is difficult nowadays to find quality electronic appliances and entertainment elements (such as speakers, DVD players, TVs, CD players, etc.) that can withstand the nigh constant jostling of being on a moving bus. All manners of electronic devices have given out on us through the years for such reasons. But even down to the simple things like bathroom hand-towel racks, the screws get jostled loose, and the contraption simply falls right off the wall and needed to be remounted. Though arduous to fix, the internal gadgets are not nearly as costly or painstaking as the external ones.

The mechanisms beneath a bus cause no end of trouble. Being that they run all year long and need to carry us to the 275 plus engagements we have in a year, they can become a problem. And when something external breaks, it isn't cheap to repair or replace.

When You Live in a Bus, Things Shift Around

And I don't mean like your carry-ons in the overhead bins on an airplane; I mean like a herd of cows in a tornado. This kind of shifting around causes single socks to inexplicably vanish, not whole pairs of socks, just individual ones. This kind of shifting around causes coffee mugs to precariously lean on the cabinet door so that when opened, they jump out like ACME anvils off a diving board. There's nothing more frightening to a young child who is climbing up on the counter by the sink to reach the high cup cabinet to get his sippy cup out than a ceramic coffee mug with the LSU Tigers' logo on it to come leaping out at him.

But other things shift as well, like the position of your food in the microwave. This only happens while we are driving, but to the inexperienced and untrained stationary person, removing food that has fallen against the microwave door while we are driving is nothing less than terrifying. And it does not help matters when the food item is particularly hot soup in a tall glass bowl—this story doesn't end well.

Not all the shifting around is the fault of the motion of the bus. A large part of it is having ten people and two laundry handlers. This creates much confusion as to whose clothes are whose.

Many a time I have found my younger brother's jeans in my drawer and had no clue as to how they got there or how long they had been in there. On several occasions I have found myself without any more dress socks and had to borrow a pair from one of my brothers, which ended up being a misplaced pair of mine anyway.

With ten people, asking someone to put something somewhere for you is not generally a good idea.

Several of the people on this bus could be considered OCD, not to a very extreme extent; but if something is out of place—cluttering a table, couch, bunk, or counter—several people will take the initiative to relocate it to somewhere more convenient for the time. And from there, the item can be moved to any number of locations on the bus and, in no time at all, wind up lost.

When You Live in a Bus, You Take Your Work with You

Loading in equipment and setting it up gets progressively easier and, in direct proportion, progressively harder as life goes on. It gets easier in that the more you do it, the more quickly you can fall into the system you have created, and it is less muscle and more method. Also, as you get older, you get stronger, and equipment is easier to load in. Conversely, as you get older, your siblings do as well, and they get married. When your siblings get married, they leave. Not always for a long time, but whenever they return, they feel a superiority by marriage that they are no longer obligated to do the work of the "family ministry".

For the last, I don't know how many, years the setup and teardown of equipment has been as follows:

Jared wakes up to find Josh already dressed and ready.

Jared gets dressed.

Jared walks outside where Josh is already loading in.

Jared opens cabinet and gets out equipment.

Jared goes to door of church and attempts to open door with equipment in hands.

Jared fails.

Jared tries again, managing to get door open with his hand just enough to slide foot inside.

Jared uses foot to kick open door as best as he can and slides through before door slams on his back and arm.

Jared proceeds to sanctuary.

Jared realizes that it would've been nice to find out where the sanctuary was ahead of time.

Jared makes a note to do this at next concert.

Jared immediately forgets note.

Jared gets to stage and sets down equipment then goes back to get more.

Fifteen minutes later...

Jared is on stage with all equipment.

Jared sets up equipment.

Jared does sound check with equipment with himself and Josh.

Jared goes to the bus to get flash drive to set up media and call people from bus in for an official sound check.

People from bus do not come.

Jared calls Mom and asks her what media she wants for that night.

Mom replies.

Jared sets up media and returns flash drive to bus.

Jared calls everyone in for sound check again.

Everyone comes.

Jared adjusts the sound for ten minutes then says it is good.

Everyone goes to bus to get changed for concert.

An hour and thirty minutes later…

Jared packs up equipment while still dressed in suit.

Josh changes in bus and comes in to haul out equipment.

Jared goes to bus to change out of suit then goes back inside to help load out remaining equipment.

All equipment is in bus, and Dad drives to the next concert where everything will repeat itself again.

The end.

For years upon years, that is what the load in and load out of equipment has been like across the board. However, there have been days when either Josh or I will sleep in, and the other will cover. Once I remember sleeping in and missing the entire Sunday morning load in. I made up for it, however, when that night I got stuck tearing everything down and loading it all in. It never happens intentionally, but it does seem like God's great equalizer that keeps us from getting angry at one another for not doing their part.

The strange thing is though I'm not the strongest guy on the block, no matter what block I live on (some of you will get that later), yet God chose me for this position, a position of heavy lifting several times a week, sometimes even a day. You don't have to be qualified to be called. You don't have to be equipped to succeed. God wants you to trust Him with everything you are, and everything you are will be enough for everything He has for you.

When You Live in a Bus, It Takes a While for Everyone to Get Ready for Anything

Now, there was some in-between time that I didn't cover in that last section. The part where we all go to the bus to change for the concert is a hectic routine that recurs as often as we do them—concerts, that is. It may not be as much of an issue for people with smaller groups who travel and sing. But when nine people live in a bus and all of them need to get ready at the same time, I don't care how many bathrooms with mirrors you have, it's not enough.

There are only three places to change on the bus: Mom and Dad's room, which is closed off with two doors that slide out from the walls to meet each other, and the two bathrooms. The back bathroom is much more spacious and convenient than any of the other places, and so it is the busiest and often the most crowded. The gigantic mirror above the sink is large enough to facilitate the faces, hair, and makeup of up to five people at one time. The standing space is limited, however; and if four others are on the floor, the fifth ends up standing in the shower.

I find it convenient that God gave most everyone in the family a particular height that allows some to see over others. In situations such as the bathroom mirror ordeal, it is a great blessing to be the tallest and be able to see over everyone else.

Let's take a tour of the old homestead. Firstly, you'll start out by taking a spiral staircase of ceramic steps up sidelong of the driver's seat, noting the cubbies for everyday shoes right in front of you, just above the steps.

As you step into the actual living space, you will find a couch on either side of you. Watch your head. There is a projector right above you, hanging from the ceiling, and a pull-down window shade mounted behind you that serves as a screen. Right above the driver seat, up near the ceiling, is a shelf with a sound bar, DVD player, TV Guardian, and a Wii with most of the accessories in a box near it. To your right is a short, two-sectioned couch that stretches from the back of the driver's seat to the countertop. To your left, a longer, three-sectioned couch starts at the edge of the steps and stretches to a small table for the younger children to eat at or for a place to spread out and work.

Behind the table is a short, single-sectioned couch that faces the windshield, and above it on the wall is a speaker for the entertainment system. Opposite this table and bench is the kitchen.

Facing the kitchen, you will see a large flat countertop and two sinks side by side and a smaller-length of countertop to the left with a coffeemaker in the background behind the faucets. A microwave/convection oven is mounted above the two sinks and bordered on either side with cabinets that span the length of the room. A similar set of cabinets are directly across from these. The cabinet on the right side stores disposable and reusable cutlery and dishes, as well as storing material: Saran Wrap, aluminum foil, Ziploc bags of various sizes, etc.

On the left side of the microwave is a cabinet that holds a wide assortment of cups: coffee mugs, hard plastic cups, and reusable refill cups from a dozen different gas stations and restaurants. Behind the bench and mounted speaker is a full-size refrigerator and freezer in which is kept everything under the sun. A pantry beside it borders the next room of the bus, the bunk room. Across from the fridge is the "half bath," a.k.a. the front bathroom.

That concludes the living room/dining room/kitchen/driver's area. I will now take you into the "bunk room". As you lay your hand on the handle of the door, it will move down a bit, a product of overuse. As you turn the handle and open the door, a creaking sound will come from its hinges. You will immediately discover that there is no light switch anywhere near the door; there is not even a good place to put one. You will find a light switch on a section of wall in between two sets of bunks in the middle of the room and to your left. As the lights come on, the first thing you will notice is the AC unit console on the wall above the switch. The second thing you will notice is the "junk bunk." This is a bunk that is haunted by the ghost of useless junk.

It once belonged to me before Caleb moved out and I took his bunk.

Directly above the junk bunk is Josh's bed. Directly below is a set of nine drawers that hold the everyday clothing for us children. On the right, across from the junk bunk are three more bunk beds. The top one was Gabrielle's before she moved out. The middle one belongs to Danielle, and the bottom one—since Gabrielle moved out and Abby took her bunk—has now come to be known as *Junk Bunk Jr.* On this bunk is kept the supplies we take to Uganda every year when we go.

Beside those three bunks is another trio of beds belonging to myself, Zach, and Christian respectively. And if you fail to grasp the significance of these beds, let me just tell you that we live in a bus full-time. Every possession we have—books, movies, toys, mementos, souvenirs, and other personal items—we keep on our beds. These beds are the one place we can claim as our own on the bus and the only place we do not have to share with anyone else.

Past the bunk room is a short hallway lined with closets. Before you get to the closets, however, there is, on your right, another bathroom. This one is known as the back bathroom, mainly because it is in the back and its doors will close both on the bathroom, leaving the hall open or, on the middle room, closing the hall off. Past this bathroom are the closets I spoke of, which end in very narrow path around a queen-size bed in the back. This also is surrounded at its four corners with cabinets. On the left (Dad's side) is the laundry cabinet; on the right (Mom's side) is the coat closet for winter coats and the like.

This concludes the tour. If you think that the bus is larger inside than it looks on the outside, you may be right. But in reality, there is only 360 square feet of space inside. The bus is home, and it will always be home. There's a lot that takes getting used to, I'm sure. But the best answer I know to give to someone who asks, "What is it like living in a bus?" is actually another question: "What is it like living in a house?" Truly, they are two vastly different worlds, and though I cannot explain my life in full, it has been the goal of this work to attempt to explain it as best I know how.

About Me

I've had a painful life, but most of it was not my fault. As a child, I was called accident-prone for my high risk of getting injured while doing nearly everything. It was rare that a year would pass by without any major injury being caused to myself, and it all started when I was four months old. As you know from the introduction, when I was four months old, my family started out in traveling evangelism. Well, before we began that ministry, a nurse of mine happened to give me the chicken pox. This accident was not my fault and did end up spreading to the other three children and my mother.

From there, the problems only got worse. When I was two, my older brother Josh convinced me that the liquid in a kerosene lamp was actually Kool-Aid and got me to drink it. Needless to say, sirens blared, and I was off to the hospital as a two-year-old to get cured of the insetting pneumonia. Again, this was not my fault. It was at my expense, but not my fault.

Well, several years passed with only minor incidents, till we were at the flagpole shop of a dear, yet now deceased friend of ours, Mr. Ed—at least that's what I knew him by. I couldn't have been more than thirteen when this next thing happened. It started with me playing out in the field by myself. Then my oldest brother, Caleb, decided it would be fun to chase me around with a rope lasso and try to hog-tie me.

I saw him coming, and I saw that devilish gleam in his eye that said, *I'm going to beat him till he's purple and then string him up* (well, it looked like that to me, at least). Caleb came charging at me, swinging the rope over his head like an idiot; and like an even bigger idiot, I ran. I ran as fast and as hard as I could, terrified of what might happen if he caught up to me. Of course, he was just playing, but I didn't know that. I was a gullible, thirteen-year-old kid.

Well, I would be running for all I'm worth, and he'd hang back a little to give him throwing room with the rope. Then I'd look back as he got closer and run harder. This went on for a while until one time I looked back; and as I turned back around, my face noticed that there was a tree inches away from it. My body was a little late to realize this, and I ran headfirst into a large, very hard tree. If you're thinking of running into a tree for any reason, I would advise against it. It is a very painful experience.

Since I was turning around when I hit the tree, my arms sort of flung out and wrapped around it. Now, not only did I have a bleeding gash right beside my left eye, I had scrapes and scratches all over my arms. However, I was not exactly lucid for those moments following my meeting with the tree; it was a very brief meeting. My face said good-morning, and the tree said good night—that was about it. Next thing I know, I'm holding my hands over my eye, leaning over the concrete driveway leading up to the back of the store where the bus is, and Mom is panicking as she runs to me.

Mothers, though. Her first move is to bring me over to the grass so that I don't drip blood on Mr. Ed's driveway—really? I love my mom.

After a short rush to the hospital and about seven stitches, I look like Frankenstein, but I'm all in one piece. Again, though, I don't see how that was my fault.

Not too long afterward, maybe a year, we were parked at Bibleville, a snowbird haven down in Texas. The people there were so nice to us kids, and every year they allowed us to use their bikes when we were there to drive around. Well, I was no older than fourteen at this point, and my legs were not quite long enough to reach the ground from the seat of one of those old school bikes that came from the good old days when they made bikes without hand brakes.

One thing to note is that my family is very competitive. When we go for a bike ride, it normally entails a bike race at some point. Now, I have fairly strong legs. It comes from being the unofficial gofer of the family. If you are unfamiliar with the term *gofer*, it's a Southern expression that essentially refers to when someone needs something, they say, "Go fer this or go fer that," which I generally end up doing.

So having strong legs, I soon gained the lead. Now, in this community called Bibleville, the vehicle speed limit is five miles per hour. I didn't know how fast I was going, but it must've been seventy or so. Anyway, up ahead there was a truck crossing the intersection horizontally. I immediately tried to hit the brakes, but it was an old-school bike. There were no hand brakes, and my feet couldn't reach the ground. So my first thought was to pedal backward. Normally that would stop the bike—not this bike. My siblings had given me the bike without any breaks.

About this time, I'd met the back end of the truck rather abruptly; and the next thing I knew, I was flying through the clouds, waving to passengers on airplanes as they passed by. Then I was falling, and falling, and falling for what seemed like hours. Finally, I hit the ground hard, apparently very hard, hard enough to knock out a tooth and simultaneously lodge it through the skin and inside my lower lip. Ouch.

Again, I don't see how this was really my fault, and I still have a tooth in my lower lip because of it.

The day after, like the moron that I was, I went bike riding again; this time, with no thoughts of speed and many thoughts of caution. As I tried to make a turn, going modestly fast, I rammed the bike into a Dumpster. Now, hitting a moving vehicle in a race, that's understandable; but hitting a stationary object when driving carefully, that is a completely different story. It took me many years to live that one down.

Most recently, I had the most bizarre and, admittedly, self-inflicted injury of my lifetime, and there have been a few.

It all started back in 2011, back in the old time. The year 2011 was before the iPhone 5, Walmart Hot-N-Ready pizza, and the Taco Bell AM Crunchwrap. We were parked outside of our old home church in Corunna, Michigan. This was where I grew up as a child, back before frosted Pop-Tarts, microwaveable pizza, and flat-screen television. It still amazes me that only ten years ago, people ate unfrosted Pop-Tarts. Look how far we've come since then.

Many summers I spent getting pelted with water balloons by the likes of Caleb Duffield and Jeremiah Napier during Arctic Camp, which was kind of like a VBS on steroids. Oh, so many fun times and good friends. Well, we were parked outside this church, and they were preparing for this year's Arctic Camp, which entailed lots and lots of water-balloon filling. And since I am officially an adult, I get to be staff rather than participant this year; meaning, I get to handle the water balloons this time. Muahaha!

Everything took place in the field behind the church; but the water spigot and, therefore, all the balloons were at the church. After the balloons were filled, they were placed in tubs and then put on the back of a truck and transported out to the field. Well, you could ride in the truck on the tailgate, or you could walk. I was feeling pretty good about myself, so I told the guys I'd just run and race them there, easy enough since they had to drive slow through the parking lot anyway.

It started off fine. I jogged beside them as we rounded the first corner of the church, but then I picked up speed a little, and so did they. Slowly I found myself being inched to the patio of the church where a row of potted plants blocked my way. Now, at this point, I had two choices: go around the plants, or jump over them. I chose to jump over them.

I cleared the first few easily and got to the very last one on the row before I messed up. Important note: the last potted plant was about six inches taller than the others, and I was at this point, so invested in this potted-plant jumping that there was no hope of aborting.

Well, as I jumped through the air, my foot caught on the plant, and I tripped. As I hit the ground, one leg buckled, and the other shot out slantways. My entire body rotated, and my ankle ended up under the front tire of a Dodge

Durango. In case you were wondering, they're actually heavier than they look.

Now, at this point in time, I didn't know if I was in shock or if I was just too lazy to shout, but I looked up at the driver and said, "Back up, back up. You're on my leg." Just as calm as calm, it was not till the other guys got out of the truck that things started to get frenzied.

One other thing I forgot to mention is this: this church right behind us was also home to a Christian school that was in session at this time. So picture this: a group of guys huddling around me and freaking out, blood streaming down the parking lot from a gaping hole in my ankle, and people running to and from the building for help and to see what was going on.

One of the guys had the thought of getting a belt tightened around my leg to stop the blood. I looked at the nearest guy with a belt, my friend BJ, who said, "It's my favorite white belt, man. I don't want to get blood on it." Down there, hands propped behind me as I leaned back, sitting and trying not to look down, I thought, *Thanks a lot, pal.* Luckily, I happened to be wearing a belt at the time, and I took it off for them to fasten it around my leg.

Moments later, one of the guys came from inside with a first-aid kit, and they pressed a four-by-four gauze pad to try and stop the bleeding. My mom happened to be in the offices of the church working on financial income books for the ministry when Josh Levesque, the pastor's son, came in and told her, "Ms. Allen, you need to come outside. There's been an accident." It was not his personality to get spastic, so he was as calm as calm could be. My mom didn't think much of it but followed him outside and saw me down on the ground and a trail of blood coming from me and just thought, *Oh no!*

This time, there was no time for sirens. I was placed in the backseat of a car and driven to the hospital. Already the pain was beginning to register, and the roads in Michigan—well, they're about as smooth as the surface of the moon.

It was like every ten seconds, a California earthquake struck. To top it all off, as we reached the suburbs to take a shortcut to the ER, a student driver pulled out in front of us and maintained speed of no greater than 4.67 miles per hour. After an eternity of driving, we arrived at the hospital where there was zero wait time for people with bloody holes in their legs. I was immediately taken to a bed where they could clean the wound.

Now, I don't mind getting run over by a truck. I don't mind the agonizingly long and painful car trip to the hospital, but the things they do to "numb the pain" are some of the most painful things I've ever been through.

First off, twenty-inch needles ought to be illegal. A needle hurts bad enough when going through an opened wound from the outside in; but when the same needle went from the inside out—may God forgive me, but some un-Christian things that I was about to do to the nurse if she tried that one more time started popping into my head. I couldn't stand it.

X-rays were rough, mostly because in order to get a picture, something had to be placed underneath my injured ankle. The motion was nauseating, but the x-rays showed no broken bones. Miracle of miracles, which I think I might have appreciated more had I not been bleeding all over the gurney at that time. I couldn't be operated on at that time, so they simply bound my entire lower leg from the knee down in a gigantic, four-inch-thick, twenty-pound, plaster-cased, quadruple-wrapped boot. Fort Knox would've been proud.

My ankle was no doubt protected, but I think my left leg is a little longer than my right now.

I returned to the hospital the next day, and the things that followed were done in a hospital gown and will not ever be spoken of again.

Well, two days and two surgeries later, I found myself bedridden; and the band played on, as the song says. The family couldn't just cancel all the bookings for the next week, and I had to stay in town for a checkup after a few days.

So Mom stayed to take care of me while the rest of the family struggled and worked to compensate for the tremendous loss of my magnificent voice. It was a terrible blow, like a body losing a head or a bird losing a wing.

I endured lying in a bed for days solid, only able to move slightly and never moving my leg more than could be helped. After a while, I made it to where I could get around on crutches, which was a blast during concerts, let me tell you.

After what was probably three or four months, I could walk again. Though it had to be done gingerly and with much caution, I soon returned to my old self again. Wiser, yes. One thing's for sure: I'll never again put on my favorite pair of shoes if there is any chance I'll be foot-racing a truck.

So maybe that was my fault, but given my history, I probably shouldn't be alive today. Those were the highlights. Many times I've come close to seriously injuring myself, and yet I live. I'm hale, I'm whole, no broken bones or serious illnesses. There must be some reason God keeps me alive—if only he didn't have to do it so often,

Another important thing you should know about me is that I am a writer. I love writing. And no matter how hard I try, I cannot bring myself to stop writing. This would not be a bad thing at all if it was not so inconvenient to be a writer while living in a bus.

> **Concentration**: a state of being focused on one object for an extended period of time without interruption.

This is impossible to achieve when on a bus that currently holds thirteen people (Caleb and his family have come back on the road with the rest of the family after a short sabbatical; hence, the change of bus population from nine to thirteen), two of whom are toddlers. For a writer like myself, concentration is one of the most vital parts of any successful writing session. But it is also one of the things you have to sometimes sacrifice when you live in a bus. Distraction is one of the easiest deterrents to create and one of the most difficult things to recover from. But this project you are reading is proof that you can be a writer when you live in a bus. It is a challenge, for sure, but it can be done. In fact, many times, my writing ideas have been spurred on by the distractions of my siblings. I could be in a mental block, and something someone says or does can completely change my train of thought and give me a fresh idea. Though, more than likely, it will make me forget about what I was writing to begin with, and I'll write something totally random in the middle of one of my sentences.

Occasionally, I will write about what someone says without even knowing that I'm doing it. I have written entire paragraphs about things completely unrelated to what I'm working on without even being aware of it because I was listening to what someone else was saying.

It's not easy being a writer when you live in a bus. Things change your train of thought in a moment. I can imagine the horrors my editor, Guy Batton, goes through in previewing all of my jumbled and disordered sentences and the random bunny trails I take—though it does make for good comedy. There was one time when I was so mentally diverted by whatever was going on in the bus that I typed an argument between myself as the narrator and my main character without even knowing I was doing it. I looked at it afterward and thought, *What on earth did I just do?*

45

Three things that are an absolute necessity for a successful writing session for me are my Bluetooth keypad, a good quantity of Dr. Pepper, and a pair of earbuds playing the Collingsworth Family, Newsong, or Jason Crabb. But when my twin nephews discover how fun it is to bang on a Bluetooth keypad and someone puts on *Adventures in Odyssey* louder than my music and all the Dr. Pepper runs out, that writing session is over.

And what is the likelihood of all those things happening at once? Surprisingly enough, about 90 percent of the time—that is exactly how it happens. It's just one of the little things that keep life interesting when you live in a bus.

When You Live in a Bus, You Get Bored

A truer statement has never been said. Being confined to a 360-square-feet space for eight hours on a long road trip is not the most exciting thing I can think of. It's only a matter of time before you have read every book you own twice or more and have exhausted your favorite playlists and CDs. There is only so much you can do while in a bus. And when someone decides to read a book and someone else listens to music, a few others are working on computers or taking naps. The options for an intellectually stimulating game or conversation are approaching nil. I'm a writer, a very avid one. But I tip my hat to the writer who can make themselves write something while they are utterly bored. To write, you need ideas, focus, and willpower. When in a bus for eight hours, driving through the wheat fields of Indiana, the only things missing are these: ideas, focus, and willpower. Not to say you can't have fun or that it's always boring. It's a blast when we decide to do something together. But on the days when we don't, you tend to get really bored really quickly.

When You Live in a Bus, You Become a Homeschooler

Being a homeschooler, I was able to surpass other kids my age and several years older in the grading system as I could take subjects on my own time and do as much of a book at a time as I could process. It was not uncommon for me to finish a three-year curriculum in a single year. This made for odd conversation when I would talk to other children my age about how tough school was, and I could actually advise them on different methods to figure out the math problems or different perspectives to approach grammar and science studies. Not to say that I was brilliant (I was), and not to say I was conceited (I was), I just had the advantage of being homeschooled.

Though, possibly the most awkward advantage to being a few grades ahead in certain subjects was not knowing what grade I was actually in overall. So when the Sunday school program at a church was divided by grade rather than age, I didn't know what to tell them. Sometimes I was in the college/seniors class; and in others, the eighth grade classes. When asked what grade I was in, I would normally tell them my age, and they would deduce what grade I should be in, or I would tell them in what class I was placed previously. I did learn a lot, and much faster than if I had been confined to a schedule. This gave me a jump-start on life and has helped me prepare for my future.

Another perk of schooling in a bus is that with the many places we visit in the United States, we do not need to take American history courses. Whenever we were in the area of an historical site, we would plan a field trip of sorts to go and learn about the person or place—places like Gettysburg, Mount Vernon, Plymouth, St. Augustine, Washington, DC, and many other widely known historical sites, as well as some obscure ones that we stumbled upon in our travels. When your life is one gigantic history field trip, who needs history books?

Being homeschooled also gave me the advantage of mixing and matching curriculums to my particular style of learning. Some subjects I retain more by reading, some by seeing, and some by writing solutions or copying information. This not only progressed the speed of my learning but the value of it.

In addition to this custom curriculum, I was also given additional studies that were geared to help me in my future goals of occupation or interest. For example, I wished to become a writer when I was old enough, and so I was given more advanced subjects on grammar, syntax, and writing theory. Even now, after I have graduated, I still am avidly pursuing this interest of mine with more poignant studies and much research. I was taught to find solutions whichever way I could. This caused my mind to develop itself to calculate in the way it was designed and process more quickly by training. I was given the freedom to learn how God made me to learn.

I've been looking for ways that a public school would have an advantage over a home school and decided that one of them is the food.

Now, I have never tried the cafeteria food at any public school but have heard stories from some of my PS friends that are nothing less than terrifying. These stories brought me to the conclusion that the cafeteria food at a public school would be a much more effective means of building up your immune system and strengthening your stomach muscles than the food at my school.

When You Live in a Bus and Are Homeschooled, You Essentially Live on a School Bus

Now, I have graduated from home school with honors. I was valedictorian of my senior class, prom queen, and finished with the highest GPA of all the Allen Home School graduates that year. Things were a bit out of sorts in my classes. We did things a little differently, not because we wanted to stand out, but because our circumstances were so different that things just couldn't be done in a normal way.

As an example of this point, my band class was one of my least favorites. I was the only member, which made practicing convenient, but I played an electric bass guitar. When you are a one-piece band composed of a single bass guitar, you don't get invited to play at many football games or anything. Besides, I was also the entire varsity team. This made not only for very dull games, but without a halftime show from the "band", and being the only person in the audience, and my own coach and play-by-play sports announcer, and the opposing team—let's just say that the sports program didn't last long.

I also had the privilege of going to school in my pajamas, which is cool, except when you couple that with the fact that I had no schedule and often woke up at eleven o'clock or later. It may not seem like it to you or me, but waking up at eleven o'clock and walking out front in your pajamas to start your school looks rather odd to the people going in and out of Walmart.

And why is that? Well, one reason might be that I live in a fishbowl. If you don't believe me, build your next house in the middle of a Walmart parking lot and make the living room entirely out of glass. When your kitchen/dining room/living room is practically just one big window, you live in a fishbowl. Now, curtains and window shades help with this a little bit, but light becomes somewhat of a necessity at some times in the morning, and the curtains and window shades to be opened to let in the sun.

About My Family

I am the fourth child in my family, the middle child. My oldest brother, Caleb, and his wife, Steffanie, live in Springfield, Missouri, with their family of three boys, my nephews. Gabrielle, my oldest sister, is married to a man named Robin, and they live in Denver, Colorado. The rest of us still live in the bus with Mom and Dad. Josh is a year older than me and sings the bass vocals for the family group, as well as being in charge of our social networking. I'm next in line, but you already know quite a bit about me. I sing lead, tenor, baritone, and on occasion, a low alto. I'm also the tech anything for the family—on stage, off stage, all day, every day. Danielle is my younger sister. She and I are the closest in age of any of the kids, being thirteen months apart. Danielle is our second soprano in the group

JARED ALLEN

and sings with Mom up in the sky on most songs. She also is the accountant for our ministry and manages the files and records. Abby is directly beneath her in age and directly above her in stature. She's the taller younger sister. Abby is the one and only true alto in our family. She likes horses, writing, books, and writing books about horses. Abby is the baker in the family. She does a lot of the cooking and such when we're on the road.

Now we come to the fun few, Zach and Christian. Zach is a die-hard Peyton Manning and Coca-Cola fan. I am a die-hard NY Giants and Eli Manning and a Dr. Pepper fan. Needless to say, such causes much competition and team pride in the house. We are a sports family. We play almost every sport—football, basketball, volleyball, golf. Soccer isn't a real sport. Being that we are from everywhere in the United States, there are several varying opinions in our household as far as sports teams are concerned. Abby likes the Baltimore Ravens. Dad likes the Saints. I'm a Giants fan, and Zach likes the Broncos. However, when it comes to college sports, we're all on the LSU bandwagon. Dad grew up in Louisiana, and that's where our Southern roots come from, so it's live-or-die LSU in our house.

It's always fun to sing in Alabama. Because they know we're LSU fans, we'll walk into a church to set up for a concert in our team shirts with "Geaux Tigers" written on the front. They'll be in their red Crimson Tide polos gloating about that one national championship game we still haven't lived down.

It's amazing that a family with so many different opinions and who are each partial to a different area of the country can be so happy together experiencing and seeing all of it. The difficulty with picking favorite states is that we've seen so much of them all to appreciate different things about different states. It is almost like picking a favorite person. Because of all the people you know and the different qualities they possess, it's difficult to pick an absolute favorite out of all of them.

When You Live in a Bus, You Avoid Conflict at All Costs

Living in a confined space limits conflict by half or more than what normal, stationary families experience. Why is that? Well, when there is no escape from the other person, you can either resolve your differences and go back to the way things were or live miserably for the next few weeks until you both forget what you were mad about to begin with.

Arguments and "fights" in our family do not end in the way you might expect. For one thing, you can't just slam the door and leave. What door would you slam? The front door is controlled by air pressure and needs to be operated by a switch. And you can't just drive away somewhere and not come back for a few days; the bus might be gone by then.

Plus, you don't have a car. So being that there is no way to stay mad, arguments dissolve rather quickly. It is tough to be angry with someone whom you live with and talk to every day. Things just get awkward when you try to avoid someone on the bus. We have found that life moves much more smoothly when you avoid conflict.

To summarize all of that, if you live in a bus, you either love each other or kill each other. The latter has yet to happen. It seems we all try to avoid unnecessary squabbles for the sake of our happiness—and overall health on the bus.

When You Live in a Bus, You Conserve Space

Every possible inch of space is utilized for storage of some kind on the bus. What we cannot fit and won't need for a long time, we keep in a room at our home church in Branson, Missouri. With all the space dedicated to storage of clothes, food items, books, and toys, there is still an overflow of things that simply have no place at all. The majority of these overflow items are kept on what is affectionately known as the junk bunk. The junk bunk is an old bunk bed that, since my brother Caleb left, has been a place to keep miscellaneous—well, for lack of a better word—junk. Where there once was a mattress, sheets, blankets, and a pillow, there now reside a printer/copier, file drawers stacked to the roof, school books in single file against one wall, and a sundry of pens, pencils, rubber bands, and manila folders.

However, the junk items are not the only things that don't have a place. There are bigger, more cumbersome items that just do not have a real storage space in which to be kept.

Shoes are a good example of this. There are closets lining the hall between the middle and back rooms of the bus, and these closets serve to store hang-up clothes, such as the things we wear on stage. Other things that can be found in the closets are clothes that wrinkle if they are not hung, and some things that are not clothes but will not fit anywhere else, like the vacuum cleaner. Dress shoes—that is, shoes for stage use—are generally kept in the base of these closets, stacked side by side and on top of each other.

The shoes we wear on normal days—as well as flip-flops and cowboy boots that are only worn on occasion but are either too filthy to put in the back cabinets or just wouldn't fit anyway—are kept in cubbies adjacent to the stairs at the entrance to the bus. With nine people living in the bus, at a conservative estimate of two pairs per person, that adds up to eighteen pairs of shoes at minimum that occupy these cubbies. With some shoes being of unusual heights, boots needing to be stored somewhere, and a lack of space in the two shoe cubbies, the steps end up with several pairs of shoes cluttering the path into the bus. It is not unusual to find marks of high heels on your boots from the many people who stepped on instead of over them when trying to get out of the bus.

When You Live in a Bus, You Spread Things

By "spread things," I am, of course, referring to illness—colds, viruses, flu. Shaking a few hundred hands a week makes it difficult to avoid catching something, especially during flu season.

We do try to stay rather healthy in the bus, drinking alkaline water, taking vitamins and supplements, and eating healthy. We consume a lot of veggies, like Larry the Cucumber and Bob the Tomato, and the rest of the gang. On a scale of fresh vegetables to frozen taquitos, we're at about a chicken pot pie, if that makes sense. We prefer home-cooked meals to restaurants. Actually, 80 percent of the food we eat on the road we cook in the fully equipped kitchen we have on the bus. However, no matter how much precaution you take, if there is something to get—with nine other people and so much interaction with so many people every week—someone is bound to come down with something. And when one of us gets sick, it's just a matter of time before we all do.

An advantage to having a large family and only four true parts to sing in a song is that someone else is on your part. This allows for one of us to get sick, but not both of us who share a part. When he is traveling with us, my oldest sibling, Caleb, sings the same part as me. But when he is not traveling with us, I carry that responsibility all alone. There have been times when I was miserably sick and yet had to stand on stage and sing because I was the only one who knew the part and could sing the part. Don't mistake me, I was not forced by anyone to do this. I did it because I love my God and believe that He will be enough to get me through it. I also love this ministry and would hate to disappoint all the people who came to hear us sing by canceling the concert just because I wasn't feeling well.

Sickness just spreads when you live in a bus, but maybe that's a good thing. That means we all get it at once instead of one or two weeks apart and have one of us always be sick.

Sickness isn't the only thing that spreads. Other things have a way of getting spread around—information, secrets, jelly. Of these three, jelly is the most dangerous. A secret on a bus is something hard to keep and will inevitably become known. Information is not often meant to be concealed, and so the spreading of it is not a big deal at all. But jelly? Jelly is a dangerous thing to get spread. No matter how many secrets you spread, there will always be more secrets to spread. No matter how much information you spread, there will always be more information to spread. But the more jelly you spread, the less jelly you will have. And while information and secrets do not require a Walmart to restock, jelly does. When you live in a bus, Walmart stops come every three to five days. Nine people can go through two jars of jelly in one afternoon. Thus, jelly being a much more precious and limited substance than secrets and information, the excessive spreading of it can lead to disaster and possibly test what I said earlier about conflict.

When You Live in a Bus, You Don't Know Where You Are From

Traveling as we do, never in one place more than a week or so, and nothing more than a home church address to tell us where our home is, how do you answer the question, Where do you live? If I answer, "Branson, Missouri," I might just as soon answer, "Uganda, Africa." We are there about as much as we are in Branson. If I answer, "The bus," then I am from whatever town we are singing in at the time. Given that this is one of those wonderfully puzzling questions, it needs to have an absurd answer. I have begun to give answers in the following manner.

> Person: Where do y'all live?
> Me: We live in our bus full-time.
> Person: So you don't have a home.
> Me: The bus is our home.
> Person: But you don't have a home you go back and forth to.
> Me: Nope. No *home*. We are homeless. He-he, actually, we live in that bus 365 days a year. Since our home *church* is in Branson, Missouri, that's where the mail goes. I guess that's where the government says I live.
> Person: Ah, so you're from Branson then?
> Me: Well, we are only there a few weeks out of the year. I suppose if we're going by that logic,

though, Walmart is where we live. We go there
more than we go anywhere else.

And there you have it. By logic and reason, I am from
Walmart. I may be the only person you have ever known
who can call his place of residence a supermarket. If home
is where you live most of the year, then Walmart is our
home. And no, you don't get a discount because it's your
home. I've tried it, and it doesn't work. Can you imagine
what that conversation would sound like?

Me: Hello, my name is Jared Allen. I live right outside
in your parking lot. Would it be possible for me to get a
discount because I live here?

What do you think that manager would say?

You also don't get discounts at Jared jewelers or Ethan
Allen furniture just because your name is Ethan Jared Allen.
It's a sad world we live in when you can't get a discount at
places that share your name.

Questions

It goes without saying that when you live in a bus, you get
asked questions.

People will always wonder about my family and how we
live in a bus, and they will always ask questions, questions
like, How do you sleep on the bus? How do you do laundry?
And how many bathrooms are there on the bus? These are
very common questions, and I answer them many times

per month. But what I'd like to address in this section are the more in-depth questions: Do you go to college? Where do you find someone to marry? These are questions seldom asked, and hardly ever are they appropriately answered. I wish to amend that with this next section.

Do you go to college?

There is actually a very simple answer to "Do we go to college?" We don't. It is not that we disagree with going to an institution of higher learning, although there are some institutions to which we do have objections. The reason we do not go to college is that, to date, none of us have ever felt a call from God to pursue a career that would require a college education and degree. In place of college, we take advanced curriculums, do apprenticeships, and pursue our dreams by practice and study.

One example of this would be my oldest brother, Caleb. He wished to become a filmmaker, so after he graduated, he went to work on sets for Christian films. In addition to the on-site training, he also purchased some films with specific worldviews to analyze and found books about the making of films. From videography, to directing, to scriptwriting, to producing, to acting, to scoring—he studied it all and added to that practical experience for other minor positions while on film sets. This is how he pursued his dream, the calling he believes God gave to him for that time.

Our callings may not always be lifelong callings. Often, God will call us to something to teach us through experience a lesson that will better equip us for what he would have us do next. So do we go to college? When it is necessary (which it has not been up to date), when it is affordable (which it has not been up to date), and when it is a wholesome, godly environment in which to learn (which it has scarcely been up to date), we will start going.

How do you find someone to marry?

This is a question that requires a very long worldview discussion before it can be answered. If I could have you, the reader, sit down with me over a lunch at Panera Bread with an hour to discuss where I stand, that would be the easiest way for you to fully understand my views on dating versus courtship, or just relationships in general. Obviously, I could not "ask a girl out" the way any other young man could. Two major reasons being that I do not have the leisure of time to get to know a young lady, much less the convenience of time to ask her on a "date." I mean, what would I even say?

"Hi, my name is Jared. You don't know me, but would you like to go out sometime? I'm in Arizona next week. We could see the Grand Canyon. Maybe take in a movie?"

No, of course not. Not only would I never approach a young woman in that way, but you can see how absurd it is for anything of that kind to happen.

It's apparent that the dating approach doesn't work for someone who lives in a bus. How about the more traditional method of courtship?

"Hello. I don't think we have met before, but I'd just like to say how much I admire you. You seem like a good, godly young lady from what I've seen in the past hour and a half. Would you agree to a period of courtship in which we would discover God's plan for both of our lives? You can pray about it, but I need an answer before I leave in ten minutes to fly to Africa for a month."

I don't know about you, but this more chivalrous approach seems even more ridiculous and unlikely than the first.

Why would any young lady in her right mind agree to something so spontaneous and preposterous? And if she did agree, would she just follow the bus around the United States and Canada to get to know me? Of course not. It would not only be awkward and inappropriate, it would also hardly be conducive to a God-honoring season of relationship that is meant to endear people to Him and then to each other.

Now that we have ruled out both dating and courtship as possibilities for getting to know someone with the intent of marriage, what's left?

Speaking for myself, I can truthfully say that, in my life, I have found that waiting is the best way to fall in love.

For those of you who just raised your eyebrows, puzzled, I'll expound.

I have done extensive biblical research on the subject of relationships between a man and a woman. After all, it's too important a decision, and too easily botched, to simply dive in without foreknowledge of exactly what you are getting into. When I said that waiting was what I believed to be the best way to fall in love, I meant it in the sense of waiting for God to bring the right one into my life. However, the promise that God will supply all our needs comes conditionally. If we simply wait for God to bring someone special into our lives and that is all we do, we've not only missed the point of trusting God with everything, but we may never cross paths with that special person. The point of waiting on God is that we make Him the love of our lives and pursue Him with all our hearts.

So in summary, when you live in a bus, you wait for God's timing and pursue Him until He brings "the one" into your life. So far, God is two for two with my older siblings' hearts, giving them to the perfect person to keep and cherish them. I trust Him with my heart as well.

Alright, now that the serious issues are out of the way, we have the question of how laundry is done when you live in a bus. With as many people as we have in this small environment, how do we know when it's time to do laundry? Where do we keep our laundry? Are there children who are "laundry kids"?

Given that the space designated for clothes in the bus is as large as it possibly can be—though it is significantly smaller than probably your own personal clothing space—and is used by nine people (though restricted to only a dozen or so outfits or combinations of), there is still much laundry at the end of one week.

Where do you keep your laundry?

In the back of the bus, on the right side of Mom and Dad's bed, is a cabinet that stretches from floor to ceiling. This cabinet contains miscellaneous hangers, laundry hampers, and whatnot. A basket for laundry resides in the floor of the cabinet but soon gets filled to overflowing.

How do you know when to do laundry?

Here are a few dead giveaways that it is time to do laundry:

- When you open the cabinet and mount laundry comes crashing down on you, you know it's time to do laundry.

- When you look in your closet and see a bunch of empty hangers, you know it's time to do laundry.

- When three of your siblings complain about being down to their last pair of socks or jeans, you know it's time to do laundry.

- When the laundry in the cabinet is piled so high that it reaches the ceiling, you know it's time to do laundry.

Are there children who are laundry kids?

You are reading the writings of one. Yes, I am a laundry kid, but I'm not the only one. When it comes time for the laundry to be washed, it is generally Danielle and myself; or Danielle, myself, and Abby who end up going to the Laundromat to do it. Once all the clothes are in and all the washers started, the three of us go on a quick drink run. Assuming the gas station or McDonald's we walk to is within a half mile of the coin laundry, we are back just in time to put everything in the dryers. That usually ends up being the highlight of my laundry day because it's not so much about getting a forty-four-ounce Dr. Pepper as as it in spending time with my two sisters.

For some reason, possibly by some conniving on my parents' part, chore day seems to always fall on the same day as laundry day. Consequently, possibly also by some conniving schemes, my parents' lunch date occurs on the same day. No one else thinks that's odd, do they?

Anyway, I don't have a legitimate reason to complain. My chores consist of beating the rugs, wiping off the dashboard, and cleaning the shower. The jury is still out on if cleaning the shower is an actual chore. I mean, it's a small room that regularly has water and soap running over its walls and floor. It basically cleans itself, so what do I do? The jury is still out on that one too. But since chore day is also laundry day, I suppose I make up for my lack of real work in chores by the hard labor of carrying laundry hampers like Santa's gift bag from the bus to the Laundromat and back again.

Stories

You can imagine that when someone has lived in a bus for twenty years—though only being conscious of that fact for about fourteen—traveling and singing in thirty-eight plus of the United States and four provinces in Canada, that said person would accumulate a good number of unusually fascinating stories. This is true. There are an innumerable amount of experiences and tales from the road that I could tell you, and there are countless more that I cannot. You meet so many people and go to so many different places that there is never a dull moment on the bus. All you need is a bit of a different perspective to appreciate the crazy little things that happen each day.

Every story has a beginning, and most of the ones that we heard as children began in the following manner:

The family was sitting in the fellowship hall of the church after a concert. Mom and Dad were talking to the pastor and his wife, who used to be evangelists "back in the day". Mom and the pastor's wife talked about how each of them managed things with children on a bus, and Dad swapped road stories with the pastor. The children did what we normally do on such occasions and helped ourselves to the sandwiches and desserts that the women of the church had set out for us. Then we went to get a front-row seat to the storytelling. The older ones would understand the stories and difficulties of travel much more than the younger ones of us, who could only hope that it was a funny story because all other kinds were too boring.

They talked about serious things for a while before they got around to the good stuff. But when the pastor's wife said, "Tell them about the time when…", it really did not matter what she said next, every one of us kids slid to the edge of our seats and focused on the pastor who was about to tell a story. Every one of us gave the pastor our undivided attention, hanging on every word he said and then laughing hysterically at the end of his story whether we thought it was funny or not. Half of the time, I don't think we even knew what he was talking about, but we laughed at it, whatever it was.

Storytelling has always been a big deal for us as we travel because everyone you come into contact with has a story. But those who know Jesus Christ as their personal

Savior have stories that are powerful renderings of God's might, which leave us speechless at the amazing love of our great Creator. Then there are some stories that are so bizarre that you can't help but laugh at them no matter how many times you've heard them before; and though I cannot tell you every story, I would like to share one of my favorite ones.

Canadian Border Patrol

There can never be enough said on this subject. It seems to be the delight of every border patrol officer to detain travelers as long as they possibly can. Though I understand their position and responsibilities, have a bit of common sense, please. I mean, what could be suspicious about a family of ten who live in a bus and sing gospel music? I think some of them enjoy the hassle they put people through, but others are genuinely concerned about doing their job and may not realize the situation in which they put travelers.

There was one time, several years ago, when our family was in the process of building a new bus. While it was being built, we could not travel in it, and we had already sold our old bus. So we rented a motor home and pulled a trailer full of sound equipment and product behind it. This arrangement worked out well until we were booked for a concert in Canada. Now, Dad is the booking agent for the family, and he is also the driver. But oftentimes he would book two events close together on the calendar that are not, by any stretch, close together on the map. This resulted in us having to drive a very long distance from wherever we were to the booking somewhere in Canada.

We drove through the night and got to the Canadian border at twelve midnight or thereabouts and were the only ones there at the time. Normally it's not a very big deal for us to cross the border, but we were in a motor home and trailer this time. Even that would not have been a problem had not the license plate on the bus been a Missouri one and the license plate on the trailer been a Florida one, and Dad's driver's license been a Michigan one. This not only aroused suspicion but provided the border patrol a reason to detain us and ask us questions.

When Dad told the patrolman that we were a Southern Gospel singing family and that we were headed to a booking, they asked if we had any product we were selling, and Dad said that we did. They asked him how much product we had, and he did not know. This was one of our first times across the border, and we had no idea what they were going to ask us, so this caught Dad totally off guard. He estimated what we were carrying under the bus, and they sent us all inside the office so they could check the bus. The waiting would not have been so bad if four of us had not had the chicken pox at the time. The hours of waiting in the office seemed to drone on forever, and Mom did all she could to comfort her four sick babies.

For about three hours, they turned the bus upside down, taking everything out from under it and creating an inventory list. Then they opened the trailer to look inside it. Dad thought, *Oh no*, because he remembered that we had a product in the trailer and he had forgotten to tell them that. Now they thought we were liars, as well as whatever else they were thinking about us.

We almost did not get through that night, but God sent a miracle. The patrolman who had been holding us, his shift ended, and a new patrolman came in who was a Christian. The man quickly understood our situation and let us get back on the bus and continue on our way, but not before slapping a fine on us for not declaring the extra product and making us pay a sales tax on all of that product.

When we finally were allowed back into the bus, we found that bags of chips had been opened and looked through. The fridge had been rummaged through, drawers opened, and there were footprints going all the way to the back room. Overall, this experience left us all with the same opinion: we *never* wanted to do that ever again.

The Day the Bus Stood Still

The best stories are the ones that can never be told to anyone outside of your own family, and every Southern Gospel music artist will agree with me on that. But there are other stories that are just meant to be shared. So if you will give me your undivided attention, I shall tell you about the day the bus stood still. Was that a play on words? Yes, it was.

It was a dark and cold night on the heels of a particularly frigid winter when our protagonists found themselves on the highway toward Odessa, Texas. The chill of the night air had reached a low of about 10 degrees Fahrenheit, which was abnormal for Texas at any time of year. This alone should have roused their suspicions to the sinister plots being woven in the dark.

The highway was deserted. Hardly a vehicle roamed its treacherous path save the dauntless bus carrying our protagonists to their next engagement. As the eight wheels of the bus rolled along the pavement of the road and the driver glanced to check the arrival time on his GPS, it happened—*pow, sputter, sputter, chug, chug, hiss, cough, screech*!

The controls went haywire, the dash lights shut down, the bus ignored all commands from the driver. Frantically, the driver searched for a shoulder or exit on which to pull over. He spotted a break in the highway divider, a median long enough to keep the entire bus off the main highway. Having no other alternative, the driver steered his vehicle onto the median and parked it there. No one in the bus knew what was wrong, but they knew they were going no farther tonight.

The driver immediately thought to contact a vehicle of sufficient torque to transport his vessel to a location of more legal and convenient position. Thus, the driver reached into his back pocket and pulled out his cellular device, proceeding presently to search the Internet for a business that would have the vehicle of sufficient torque that he sought. He then engaged in contacting each of the eligible businesses to see if they would send a vehicle to remove his bus from its current location. However, in the night, when it is 10 degrees, it is rather difficult to bring oneself out of a warm bed to tow a large bus. So there was nothing to be done about it that night.

Something was wrong with the bus, and though we didn't know what it was, the bus was not going anywhere. The driver—that is, Dad—called the church we were singing at in the morning and told them of our predicament. Members of the church who were only thirty or so minutes away brought a church van to where the bus was parked on the highway median and left it there for us to use to get to church in the morning.

So in recap, there is now a bus and a church van parked on a median in the middle of a highway in Texas. This aroused some police attention. An officer approached the bus and inquired as to what was going on. Dad explained and was told by the officer that he couldn't leave the bus parked there. We were told to try and find a wrecker with a truck capable of pulling and moving us somewhere more convenient. However, we had already done that, and after the officer made a few calls of his own and discovered that there truly was nothing to be done about it until morning, he allowed us to remain there that night without another word.

In the freezing weather, at seven o'clock in the morning, Josh, Caleb, Dad, and I loaded our equipment into the church van that was left there the night before and drove thirty minutes to the church to set up. Then we drove back to the bus to get dressed and ready. When the entire family was dressed, we drove the van to the church and made a call to get someone to tow the bus to the church as we were in concert. The bus ended up in the shop that afternoon where we learned the problem. The transmission had blown, and it would eventually cost us sixteen thousand dollars and four weeks in a van and trailer before it was fixed. Many stories happened in between the time the bus broke down that night and the time when Dad, Josh, and Caleb drove back to Odessa, Texas, from Florida to pick it up. But that is the story of the day the bus stood still.

Though I said I was going to tell you about the day the bus stood still, in reality, there have been many days like this one. Like the time the engine blew out, and we traveled in a truck and minivan, or the time we had the bus remodeled and lived from a hotel to a friend's house to a hotel. They are few and far between, but setbacks of this size do exist, and except for the grace of God, this ministry may never have survived them. The truth is, storms happen; and if we have to take a van and trailer around the country for six weeks every three years, so what? It's just something that happens when you live in a bus.

Home Sweet Bus

In the late spring of 2014, a film crew from Stiletto Television came to film my family for a pilot episode of the new TLC series, *Home Sweet Bus*. Now, Stiletto is a production company. It is their job to film all the footage, compile it into a show, and send it to the network. Let me back up a few months and explain how all this came about. Well, in the late months of 2013, our family received an e-mail from Stiletto TV, asking for more information about our family, as they were considering us for a show on Nat Geo (the National Geographic channel). At first, we thought it was spam, wouldn't you? But we checked it out, and the company looked legitimate. So we responded back to them and asked what types of things they would like to know. After several weeks and several videos of us as a group, responding to questions and comments from Stiletto, things began to move forward.

Much of those first weeks of acclimation were for informative reasons, but they also established our personalities in the minds of this production company. After we gave them everything they requested, there was a period of waiting, when Stiletto pitched the idea of our family to several networks and awaited their responses. Their original reason for finding our family was for a Nat Geo show about traveling and experiencing different cultures and areas of the United States. Our family didn't fit that description very well, so Nat Geo decided to look in other areas. However, the production company still liked the idea of what was at the time thirteen people living in a bus, traveling and singing full-time.

So they tried a few other networks, and eventually, TLC picked up the show. Stiletto formed a film crew to film the first episode of what was to be a series of shows on TLC. Well, if you've watched this show or have followed our family recently, you'll know that *Home Sweet Bus* never made it past the pilot episode. However, the time that the film crew was with us added an entirely new dimension to life in the bus because now, there was not just the thirteen of our family traveling on the bus. When we were filming, there was a producer and a PA in the back room, a sound engineer in the middle, and two cameramen with shoulder-mounted cameras in the front with all of us. It was very tight quarters to say the least.

People ask us how we liked it or how it was to have cameras follow us around all the time. It was definitely a unique experience, waking up at nine o'clock (which is an insane and ungodly hour for a traveling artist), strapping on a mic pack first thing, and then knowing that there were two guys with cameras and three mounted GoPro cameras watching your every move. Just the fact that anything and everything you said and, likewise, every action or motion could be recorded was a very scary thought. By the end of the day, even though we hadn't really done any work, we were very tired, mostly because of the subconscious efforts we made to ensure we didn't slip up and say or do something we'd regret.

But this filming was a good time for us. Many of the crew became our friends in no time at all. I can still remember all their names and faces as if they were still here. We liked each other, but more importantly, we loved them and tried to show them God's love. So if nothing else came of that one episode, at least these few filmmakers would see God's love in us.

But that wasn't all that came out of it. That one episode exploded with popularity the first day it aired. Albeit it caught a lot of views for being directly after the Duggar wedding, it did very well for a pilot. Over 1.6 million households tuned in to the show the first time it aired. TLC re-aired it on the following Monday, and it received another 500,000 views. Our family website exploded in hits in the first few hours of the premiere, and several bookings for our ministry resulted from that one episode. God did great things through that one episode on TLC, and I'm sure will use it for many great and awesome purposes to further His glory.

Stuck

One of the most awkward things I think that we've ever had happen to us in all our travels happened not too long ago. We were driving late on a Saturday night to the church where we would be singing the following morning. We had been to this church many times, so Dad knew the way fairly well and therefore didn't employ the use of GPS for direction. It was late, and this was right after the bus had been wrecked. Wait—let me back up a bit here.

A few weeks back from this time, we were on our way to our first Christmas concert of the season in Rushville, Illinois. While driving down the road in a routine way, the truck in front of us decided to stop and turn much quicker than a twenty-ton bus can stop. So, going about fifteen miles per hour, Dad tried to turn into the left lane to avoid crashing into the guy. Well, the guy in the truck happened to be turning left, and the right corner of our bus connected with his backside, shoving him off into the ditch on the left side of the road.

We pulled over to the left side because the shoulder on that side was wide enough to accommodate the bus and we wanted to check on the guy and his truck. Thank heaven no one was hurt on either side. But the impact of the crash shattered our right windshield, bent the front frame, and broke the door hinge so that the door hung cockeyed in the frame. It was an awful mess, but we still had a concert to get to. So after everything that could get cleared up at the site of the accident was cleared up, we drove on—broken windshield, cockeyed door, and everything else still plowing down the highway. My brother Josh and I had to take turns sitting on the steps and holding the door shut so it wouldn't fly open while we were driving. It was awful.

Long story shorter, we made it to that concert and then traveled on from there. We couldn't do anything about it at the time as we still had bookings to fulfill, and the bus was and is our home—we couldn't just leave it, especially since the door wouldn't close. Being that the door didn't close, for security reasons, I slept out front on the couch for the next several nights, just in case.

Anyway, fast-forwarding back to my story, we were driving. It was late, the door still wouldn't shut, and we were all very tired. Around midnight, Dad missed the turn for the church, and we were about a half mile away. Well, this wasn't Dad's first rodeo. He had missed this turn before, and there was a church ahead with a large field out front where we usually turned around. It is important to note that this area had been getting a lot of rain recently and that the ground was softer than normal.

So at twelve midnight on a Saturday, we sunk into the ground in the front yard of a church we weren't even supposed to be at. We got out and looked at the front tires. They were buried in six inches of thick mud, and we knew it was going to be a long night. Our first thought was to find something to dig with around the church to see if we could dig our way out. Unfortunately, this church must not have this problem very often; thus, there weren't any digging materials to be found. What we did find were stacks of bricks, which we used to build a ramp of sorts behind the tires.

Picture this: Late in the night, a giant bus is stuck in the mud in front of a church. Four guys are on their hands and knees in the cold, digging with a rebar pole and a large wrench and placing bricks around the front tires of the bus. Well, we tried for a while, and nothing worked, so Dad called up a friend who was from the church we were supposed to be at tomorrow morning, and he came with a couple of guys and a small tractor to help pull the bus out. Well, the tractor couldn't budge the bus an inch, and the backup plan had to be employed.

An hour later, a bulldozer arrived and was able to pull the bus out with no problem at all. We ended up at the church with a little bit of sleep and sang the next morning, wondering how the faces of the congregation from the other church would look after finding large tire tracks and indentions in their front lawn the next morning. It was a crazy night to say the least.

When You Live in a Bus, You Meet a Lot of People

People come in all shapes and sizes, from a variety of backgrounds and from all different countries. Though I haven't met them all, obviously, I have met a large variety of them. Some of the most interesting people I've met in my lifetime are not extraordinarily talented singers, songwriters, dancers, or even ministers of the gospel. In fact, some of the most incredible people I have ever had the privilege of knowing are those who possess no extraordinary gift at all. In their weakness, God has shown Himself strong time and time again to those who have trusted Him and know what it feels like to be close to Him.

My family has, for nineteen years, operated our ministry on a faith basis, never asking anyone other than God to provide for our needs—and He always has. Those who know Jesus Christ can testify that He is why they do what they do, even if what they do is package groceries in a supermarket.

> Whether therefore ye eat, or drink, or whatsoever ye do, do all to the glory of God. (1 Corinthians 10:31)

God is the reason we do what we do, but the people we meet make it fun. Not everyone has to be the best in the world at something. You have been given a talent and a gift by God, and even if you don't see it yet or realize it, God wants you to use the talent for Him. Whether you live in a bus or in a house, He wants to use you to bring glory to Him.

When You Live in a Bus, You Have a Different Perspective on Life

Perspective is an interesting thing. If I can shift your point of view 180 degrees, I will have flipped your world upside down. Here are a few viewpoint-shattering answers to a few seemingly simple questions.

What do you do for a vacation when you live in a bus? Well, a road trip is out of the question. That would be like you deciding to go back and forth on your commute to work for your vacation. So no road trip.

What about flying or taking a cruise to a tropical island or beach resort? Can you imagine the cost of airfare for thirteen people to go to the Bahamas? And you have to also take into account that my family takes annual mission trips to Uganda, Africa, and have also visited Jamaica, London, Zambia, Botswana, Namibia, and Guatemala. After you have been on a mission trip, you never look at the resorts without looking behind them at the poverty-stricken streets. Okay, so no road trip and no flight to another country.

What about a theme park? This is a better idea than the others but also must be discarded in light of the fact that we sing at theme parks often and have been to the best of them already as performing artists. There is some excitement in theme parks, but why pay to go somewhere that you will get in free later on in the year?

You are probably wondering something similar to, *What on earth do these people do for a vacation?* Well, my idea of a good vacation is having time to spend with my family and, ironically enough, working on my writing. It's how I relax.

Vacation is not a matter of getting go to exciting places or experience new things. It's about taking time off from work to spend more time doing the things you love and enjoying those you love by spending time with them.

What do you do for fun on a normal day? In contrast to the previous answer, this one will likely be mind-blowing because of how closely it aligns with your own hobbies and relaxing routines.

All of us enjoy sports. Some of us are more "into" sports than others, but we all participate in games of basketball, football, and volleyball. One of the benefits of having a large family is always having enough players for most any sport we all want to play. Because we live in a bus, we never lack a means to participate in a sport. Either a church will have a gym with a basketball court, or a large field with room for football, or a volleyball court on the grounds, or a park close by. We could even make due with a soccer goal as a makeshift volleyball net.

Besides playing sports, most all of us enjoy watching them. Golf is one of the favorites, and everyone seems to have a favorite player. Dad likes Phil Mickelson, Caleb likes Rory McIlroy, Abby's favorite is Rickie Fowler, and Zach likes Bubba Watson.

We are all team players, so when someone suggests we play football or whatever it may be that day, we all jump on board with the idea.

I am fond of reading books or studying the Bible with the time I have to spare. Or sometimes I will attempt to write a song. But for the days when we are driving, a travel version of Scrabble or Boggle is the general fallback. Even Scattergories is taken out every now again. As I said before, there is never a lack of things to do on the bus, just a lack of desire to do them.

When You Live in a Bus, You See a Lot of God's Beautiful Creation

Not a week goes by that someone does not ask one of us children, What is your favorite state? It's hard to give an honest answer to such a question because none of us have a bias for any of the states, and very few of us have any reason to have a prejudice against any of them. We consider them all to be our home, and since our family and friends are spread out all over the United States, we find it difficult to have to choose any one over another.

It's hard to pinpoint a single favorite state because we like the climate but dislike the lack of greenery, or we may favor a state because we know people who live there but are not very partial to the weather. There are so many variables to be considered that the discussion of favorite often comes down to experiences we've had in each of the different states.

I'm not particularly fond of the area of South Texas, not because of the people or the weather so much as the dryness. It seems I'm allergic to that area, as well as parts of Arizona. At least, that's what my nose tells me. It does not like it when I go too far south, and it randomly starts bleeding. But this is just another one of those little things that happen when you live in a bus. I've always been a fan of cold weather and have often said I'd rather freeze to death than burn to death. In fact, I like cold weather so much I will pretend it's cold even when it isn't. I get really excited when a cold breeze comes through on a warm day.

Though it is not possible for me to physically change my circumstances, I can pretend like they do not exist. For instance: I want it to be winter all year, and so I wear my trench coat in the summer. No matter how much I act like it is winter, and no matter what I do to convince others that it's winter, will that make it become winter? No, it will not.

And yet people all over the earth try all their lives to convince themselves and others that they are Christians and are good with God. But acting like a Christian will not make you one. My dad often says that going to church won't make you a Christian any more than standing in a garage will make you a BMW.

So why do we try so hard to fake being something we are not? A large part of it is being unwilling to let someone else rule your life for you. This is something I don't get. I look back on the few short years I have lived, and all I see is what a terrible mess I have made of my life. If I am incapable of getting it right, why do I so obstinately refuse the only one who is incapable of getting it wrong?

That doesn't have much to do with what I was talking about; but hey, when you live in a bus, you have a lot of time to think—about life, about God, about everything. I hope you don't think I wrote this little book just to tell a few stories and, hopefully, get a few laughs. I wrote this to show you that even someone who has every possible thing to hold him back or distract him from using the talent God has given him can still be successful in what he believes he has been called to do.

The bus is possibly the worst environment in which to attempt to be a writer. Without God's help, I would never be able to do it. Actually, without God's help, I would probably go insane. But it doesn't matter who you are or where you are. As I've tried to show you through this book, we are not that different, me and you. If God can make a writer out of me, then nothing is impossible with His help.